Selected Poems

Selected Poems

Joseph Langland

THE UNIVERSITY OF MASSACHUSETTS PRESS

AMHERST

Designed by Susan Bishop
Set in Linotron Sabon by Keystone Typesetting, Inc.
Printed and bound by Thomson-Shore

Library of Congress Cataloging-in-Publication Data

Langland, Joseph.
[Selections. 1991]
Selected poems / Joseph Langland.
p.   cm.
ISBN 0–87023–747–0 (alk. paper).
I. Title.
PS3562.A5A6   1991
811'.54—dc20   90–24604
British Library Cataloguing in Publication data
are available.

*Frontispiece portrait of Joseph Langland,
courtesy of Jack Coughlin.*

for Judith,
Joseph Jr., Elizabeth and Paul

CONTENTS

ACKNOWLEDGMENTS

The following poems have been previously published in earlier collections.

In *The Green Town* (Scribner's, 1956): Song with Bells, Willows, The Serpent, Wood Pitch, Ecclesiastes, A Little Homily, The Cobra, War, A Sea-Change, Dry Grass, Winter Juniper, Fall of Icarus, Hunters in the Snow, Henri Matisse, A Madrigal: For Judith, Rocky Mountain Snowstorm

In *The Wheel of Summer* (Dial Press, 1963): Second Principles, Crane, Sacrifice of the Sparrows of the Field, The Wheel of Summer, A Love for God, Buchenwald, Near Weimar, Rock, Ballad of Poor Will, Schweitzer, Sacrifice of a Rainbow Trout, Sacrifice of Gophers and Woodchucks, Sacrifice of the Golden Owl, Sacrifice of a Gunnysack of Cats, Sacrifice of My Young Mare, Great with Colt, Sacrifice of the Old Gentleman, Sacrifice of the Old Sow, Sacrifice of Eric, Sacrifice of Aunt Marie, The Amalfi Grotto, Upon Hearing Three Hundred Children Singing, Libertyville, Among Olive Groves

In *The Sacrifice Poems* (North American Review Press, 1975): Sacrifice of the Dandelions

In *In The Shell of the Ear* (MR Brochures, 1977): The Soul Hears Its Country Childhood Singing Near the Edge of Town

In *Any Body's Song* (Doubleday, 1980): Dandelion, In the Shell of the Ear, Upon the Origin of What Really Matters, Lost Faces, Any Body's Song, Getting Ready to Really Leave, Norwegian Rivers, Winter Nights in the Land of the Midnight Sun, Intimations of the Ordinary Truth, Song at Evening, My Own Country, Conversations from Childhood, Trilliums Hepaticas, and Wood Lilies, Singing in Late Summer, The Lotus Flower, A Hiroshima Lullaby, A Stone for a Maker, A Little Day Music, Holding Them Still, Windflower Songs: For Harvey Swados, In 1912, My Father Buys the Victor Record of "Sextet from Lucia," Ballad in a Summer Season, Sibelius, A Dream of Love, Walden

Many of these poems appeared first in periodicals, including: *Accent, Amherst Record, Atlantic Monthly, Chicago Tribune, Christian Herald, Epoch, Gob Pamphlets, Harper's Bazaar, The Hudson Review, Listen, London Magazine, Massachusetts Review, The Nation, New Mexico Quarterly, New Orleans Poetry Journal,* New World Writing, *The New Yorker, North American Review, Northwest Review, The Paris Review, Perspective, Poetry: A Magazine of Verse, Poetry Northwest, Prairie Schooner, Prism, A Review, Quabbin, Saturday Review, Shenandoah, Spectrum, Virginia Quarterly Review, Western Humanities Review, Western Review,* and others.

Ten to fifteen of the poems have been set to music and many have been reprinted in texts, readers and anthologies.

I

The blood
wanders the blue arterials
into the veins of earth.

In the Shell of the Ear

for Judith

Your warm skin is an old road under my hands
as mine in yours. If I have wandered
deep in the cave of your ear,
then hear me out in my watery songs
while your fronds of hair
wave like lilies over the traveled sea.

Though body aches, body is lovely still:
music of muscle,
timpani of bone,
reeds and the gut-strung frets of mind.
Wound to a pulse of bellows, the blood
wanders the blue arterials
into the veins of earth.
If the heart, that live volcano,
troubles the soft and lost subcontinents
for love,
let it burst, at last, if it must.

Somewhere an old horn blows, forever new,
by a dark cave filled with numinous passages
that feed, at last, upon this ancient sea.
The blood rises,
it floods the body's shore
and congeals to grains of salt on a bed of sand,
asleep in the ear of Circe, like a shell.

Dandelion

Yellow, yellow, yellow,
weedy and earthy and juicy dandelion,
I love you, giving wings
to your dark seed, clouded with silver hair,
suspiring to your natural desecrations.

Now, in this place,
after that plush and velvet heart
gives up its character,
I feel that you are always arriving
by wandering where you will
in any wind.

Yours is a bitter root and a stout stem.
Strength by strength,
have I not gathered your deep white sockets
into my galvanized buckets
and banked them with my daily fires?

You are both a small sun
and a pale moon.
When you come
flowering through the daylight
my blood smiles in its skin;
and under any moons that I have known
those disembodied hosts of stringent mouths
still populate these bones.

Breathing that fragrance now,
something expires.
But even if you rose and turned and went
memory would keep you
rampant on its green and golden bed;
and even then, given a little time
while loneliness distills the weedy ground,
you would still be this clear white wine
sweet to my tongue,
where all these windy words and ghostly throngs
have, in your absence, come.

Upon the Origin
of What Really Matters

for Julie and Lois

And,
after a long journey,
we rose upon the pure white breast of winter
    (O child, children)
in the fallen dusk of sun
tunneling into the moon.

There,
in Highland Township meadows,
a pine tree, somber in its head of boughs,
    (blue-green, gold)
drooped crystals from its stems
and called our shadows in.

Something
familiar in its arms
fragrantly lifted; it whispered to the dark
    (starlight, starbright)
distance of sheds and barns
and ringed that forest field

with dreams
of strange illuminations.
But whether music, magic, games or stories
    (forget, forgetting)
or the gnomes of old desires,
we all, it seems, forgot.

And
plunging through the snow
we came, once more, along those playhouse roads
    (hello, hello)
upon men, women, and homes,
and a huge grave of songs.

Lost Faces

Then,
turning the corner of our little town
in southeastern Minnesota,
I came upon your face, aloft in light,
held to a shadowed angle in the sun.

I had never met you before, never in all the world,
but there you were, there in my little town,
as though you had always been
walking there up and down.

Nothing seemed out of place,
your dress, your hair, the color of your eyes,
the contours of your face.
It was so natural, so absolute a grace
that there was no surprise . . .

only, by chance,
some recognition in your glance
that parted my lips to say hello
to someone I had never known.

You seemed, at once, a neighbor to my heart
and made a usual day of wind and sun
with white clouds drifting in the sky
so strangely local that we seemed to step
right from the sidewalk to each other's arms,

although we only paused
a second at that corner there, no more,
and barely touched each other, passing through a door
of shade and sunlight, hinged upon our hands,
took a few troubled steps,
looked backward, but at different times,
and went on to our private lands.

It was as though the quickened heart had sent
a frontier expedition from its breast
across the Mississippi, going west,
and rode the far Dakotas, mound and plain,
two thousand miles of wilderness and rain,
while all the sky
abstracted in its own renown
to one blue eye,
sent back into my life and to my town
only its mute report,

as though eternity had made a stop
somewhere west of the mountains where the mind,
body and heart,
might sit on a sunny headland, gazing out
past rock and wave and mist of what we are and seem
upon the blue Pacific, like a dream.

Any Body's Song

Here's an acorn from my breast;
plant it gladly, let it rest.
Lie down in its broken shade,
body out of sunlight made.
And if any twig or leaf
fall upon your summer grief
let it root upon the mind
while I catch the autumn wind.

If some little chill should kiss
fingers that my lips did miss,
put your warm hand on my heart
where those chilly rumors start.
If we lie here easy now,
cheek to cheek and brow to brow,
let your sweetly troubled eyes
hide and think our body wise.

Come in to my arms and grow
into me before the snow
takes our warmth and all our good,
frozen, to a winter wood.
Be a shadow for the sun;
be a bough across the moon.
Whisper now above the sound
of dry leaves dropping on the ground.

Take me from these new alarms;
be a lute upon my arms.
Tell me, for the body's sake,
song and lute and heart will break.
Though it bring disaster soon,
I would tremble in this tune
till our bodies rise and fade
downward to another shade.

Somewhere in another wind
lives the lady of the spring;
let her come and teach me grace,
brush her lips upon my face.
Memory tells me solitude
tells a riddle to the blood;
let my heart obey, as well,
beat and heartbeat, like a bell.

If, by chance, I touch your hand
somewhere in another land,
if I knock upon your door
somewhere in another world,
let this oak abide us there,
lift its boughs upon the air.
And let your summer shadows run
through me till our time is gone.

Getting Ready to Really Leave

Then, gathering in the dusk,
comes the strange long possibility of loneliness.
Some simple rolling tune invades the dark,
routing all that nostalgic poise
of half shadows.
He stands, alone in an open room,
listening.

A moth beats at the rusted back-door screen;
a stray car hums in another street.
Old songs, old songs:
someone is going; someone is going away . . .
And then that tune, like a sentimental favorite
waltzing mindlessly around the years of young nights
and floating over the glamorous local stages
of county fairs,
trembles once more,
follows an echo further down the street,
falters, fades in again,
and is gone.

We swing for an utter moment upon that hinge—
hello, Somebody—
hover, ever so briefly upon that porch,
impersonal as the summer air,
and move on out
into the perfect silence of the town.

Norwegian Rivers

for the sesquicentennial of Norwegian
immigration to the United States, 1975

Yah, they are so kind of restless,
rushing around hills
and tumbling the polished stones;
they always have somewhere to go.
Even when they pause in precipitous valleys
they climb
into deep long cold lakes
and then again begin
rapidly falling.

Yah, we have seen them
pouring off mountaintops
like the first dream of a second flood.
And now, one hundred blood years later,
they amaze Norwegian-American travelers,
sailing the birdlike ferries
toward the evergreen towns
or running through summer on the cliff-hung roads
with the sheer bravado of their origins.

Yah, now shall they see,
the affluent grandchildren,
how strong and supple minds
ran those rebellious rivers into the sea.
And now, yah, shall they hear
the low music of springs
watering those impoverished mountain meadows.
Then let them guess as they can,
yah,
how the terrible excitements of alienation
fell on the manhood of our great-grandfathers
and the playfulness of their children,
then rose in a heartbreaking cry from their limbs
and washed from their empty hands.

Then, yah, it was then,
stout in their sadness,
they stuffed their childhood into rosemaler trunks,
clamped them with iron bands
locked once and for all on the eastern hemispheres,
and down those rutted trails and noisy rivers,
out through the western fjords,
they rode for half a century over the Atlantic
on one great ascending wave
toward the virgin hills and the wide inland valleys
of Iowa, Minnesota, and Wisconsin.

And now, yah, even now,
grandmothers sitting in their rocking chairs
and watching their children's children
in Bergen and Decorah, Hardanger and St. Paul,
say, half to themselves,
yah, they are so kind of restless,
they always have somewhere to go,
hearing under their vaguely troubled
half-drooping eyelids
the melancholy of those hard hills
and those old stones,
and rivers calling under the walled-up fjords
to the muffled horns of the sea.

Winter Nights in the Land of
the Midnight Sun

*for Trygve Larsen and Knud Hammervold, upon being
given a home for the night with them in Kautokeino,
North Norway, after traveling with some Laplanders and
a herd of 2,000 reindeer*

Cloudberries rise from the snow,
and black crows, feather-thin;
    dwarf branches hone
    cold rime in gold;
Reindeer-Lapps run in their skins.
All sway to mountainous viddas in Finnmark and in Troms.

We arrive, far up, unknown,
a friend, perhaps, of a friend,
    and may go, who knows,
    each one to his own,
and each to his polar end,
never, no never, ever, to gather our hands again.

Or maybe, to meet the mind
calling back something it knew
    whenever the wind's
    strange discipline
swings almost true-north true
on Alta and Lyngen fjords its long deep thought of you.

Or else, when gratitude,
tried in its loneliest place,
    learns that our blood
    need not be rude
in any such alien place,
endures, and becomes familiar, taught to a different face.

Then every door and street
is like your own home town,
    its hills complete;
    our rivers meet
and flow, together, down
into those great wild seas, conversing underground.

By chance, so might we too
have been merely traveling on
    over longitudes
    and up latitudes
where we just might never have come.
But then we smiled and met, and sat down in your home.

Intimations of the Ordinary Truth

for F. W. T.

Yes,
we have heard you whispering at the edges of our houses
in Amherst, Massachusetts,
or standing aloof, questioning sleep
and the drowned harps of the sea.
And now in your tides of surrounding shadows
you are still waiting, turning in blurred rings,
engulfing our watery eyes.
You,
with your great and enigmatic brow
flashing by fires and swords and masked sentries
in the stony frieze of the ages,
we have seen you wither away into genies
in the open palms of our friends;
you,
falling the long trajectories of God
into the brass mouths of bugles,
we have tripped your barreled eye
and heard your polished bell.
Once,
you came at dawn through the meadows of Wyoming
to brush your casual lips upon our temples;
and once,
in a gust of wind near Decorah, Iowa,
we heard, or thought we heard,
your great subtle hooves falling away toward evening
when a few stray raindrops
pocked and powdered the dusty roads;
and once,
at high noon in the chilled and rocky streams
you lay for a moment in the riffles of brushed water,
but when I reached out with my hand
only a mossy stone came dripping to the sun.
And once,
in La Crosse, Wisconsin,
you loafed at a street corner, a dark stranger,
awaiting only a brief nod,

and, once in a blue moon, a swift embrace
before the lights went down upon that inland river
and slept in all its radiant streams
upon the Gulf.

Beyond those waters, beyond these brooks and tides,
beyond the Caribbean,
adrift in other seas,
this old imagination rides its tough and ghostly sail
on the ring of our blue sphere,
as though by holding a small stone in our palm
we began, far off, to understand
the Alhambra or Angkor Wat,
Chartres or the Taj Mahal or the Parthenon.

There, here now, and everywhere,
these misty proclamations on our tongues
riot our days and nights
and fire us all with immediate history.
The wandering stranger at nightfall
follows the street we all went up and down,
stops with his ear to our homely doors
and knocks. And listens.

The heart rocks and glistens on that shore.

And into the shadow and inner shade of ourselves
we fall, we fall, we fall
like prayer;
while, sure as Sunday, in the old forbidden cities
and the greening mud flats under our broken towers,
we hear that faintly echoing bell,
fired in hills of trees and stones,
kissing the common air.

Song with Bells

Once in childhood's rainwater wells
Sunday sounded
Sky-clear, sun-bright, rounded
As fabulous piping in fluted sea shells

Over long green hills of ocean swells.
Day was a sinewy flowing,
Brass glowing
Through bing-shaped, bang and bong bells.

Somehow insistent beating of bells
Trembles our history, crying
Epiphanies danced into dying.
We assume what tone tells.

If grief grins or laughter knells
For children skipping and calling
Toward ancient teardrops falling,
Weep and laugh also. Love is a lonely

Somehow insistent beating of bells.
Fluted in sea shells
Love equally tells
Dead-man blues and bridegroom bells.

Second Principles

When you say that the moss-rose harbors a juicy stem
And gathers its moisture out of the arid air
And thrives in a blazing sun, what have you said?

You have said that the object exists and is worth attention.
That you gave it attention and found it worthwhile to report
That the moss-rose under the sun has a juicy stem.

You have said that the parts of creation are many and strange,
That we follow them, one by one, in a greenwood hope
That the sum of their parts is, itself, a significant record.

You have said that the sun cannot wither this miracle dry,
And that haunted with miracles men find it useful to go
Hunting in the universe in search of their identities;

You have said that they sometimes find it among the rocks,
Nature a naked psychology under their eyes,
The ironies of cool behavior under their senses.

So coolness can come, you have said, from a crown of fire,
Water out of the sun, tenderness out of the stones.
Even dun circumstance flowers upon the world

If you are there to watch it, if you report it,
If in reporting you grant it a color of mind
And a color of language. There on the blazing rock

The moss-roses gather sweet nectar into their stems,
Rounding and waxing their leaves and blossoms of flame.
There's one! And look, there's another! Another! Another!

Willows

Willows are trees of life. They ride
Their limp boughs to their feeding ground
And sound
Their roots in their immediate countryside.

Like them, I, too, survive
By circular and seasonal disguise;
One golden childhood willow kept my eyes
In a huge green honey hive;

Those twigs and saplings of indifferent dreams
Blooming upon their mountain meadowlands
Sprang in my hands
Like shadows on the upper willow streams.

Now down they run like water to broad plumes
Of delta beds
And toss their palaces of tangled heads
In green felicities of trailing rooms

While rivers in the silted sands dispute,
With sea-borne gravity,
The overflowing tree,
The plunging siphon root.

That thirst would drink the creek beds dry:
Or so I thought. But minnow schools
Sparkle in willow pools,
Shifting their golden flecks in that bright eye.

So have I lain in depths while vision pearled
Over the clouded surfaces of things
In dense imaginings
With one eye squinting upward into the world

Out of my willowy sleep. That memory calls
Where the old willow tells
Of disembodied cities of floating bells
Tumbling simultaneously through waterfalls.

The spring floods flash. Believe me, one can not
Casually remember now
All jewels hidden under the willow bough,
In all begetting time what one begot.

When I am an old man and dying, almost lost
On the northern slopes of death, a stiff reed
Trembling from husk to seed,
My flutes all cracked with frost,

I will translate myself into a brown
Paradise of willow roots, a whole
Country of mountain meadows for the soul
Dreaming toward natural grace in a green town.

The Serpent

The hooded reptile, in his guile,
Knows how to dance and how to smile.

Some say he merely writhes and grins
Through solemn subtleties of sins,

But look, his jeweled body turns
To rings and bracelets in the ferns.

He grazes on the velvet grasses
With coral feet, then dewlike passes

Flickering on the darkling ground
In neural sandals of no sound.

Glimpsed at the lily pool, he glides
Serene among its undertides

And wakes soft ripples into bells
Of water sepulchered in shells;

So kissed, he resurrects his head
Above the broad-leafed lily bed

And blasts the ivory blooms among
Pale whispered powders of his tongue.

Standing in water like a spring
Long-coiled for Satan's underling,

Spinning through subterranean loves,
Feeding upon pure lily groves,

He makes an ikon with his thin
Needle of spiraled medicine.

Seductive, convoluted, poised,
He equals elements, unvoiced

Except for one hushed song of death,
A sudden exodus of breath.

And now he floats and slides and soars,
Glistening, upon the further shores

And waves toward Calvary, his gloss
All intersected in a cross;

There, hung in haloes, all amazed,
So slyly caught, so subtly praised,

Fleeing among his purple stings
Love dances, smiles. Oh, how he sings!

Crane

One day when childhood tumbled the spongy tufts
Banking the naked edge of our bottomlands
A shadowy sand-hill crane
Arose from Rocky Spring with a flipping fish,
A speckled rainbow,
Speared in her slim black bill.
She offered her wings in sluggish waves,
Wading impossibly up the slapping waters,
And ascended the crystal floods.

Under that dark ark
Two grappling anchors of dangling legs
Rolled away so smoothly the eye forgot them
Until that tall ungainly crane
Lay in the sky like a dream.
Her snaking head
Pivoted vaguely over our deep, green valley
And straightened to kiss the horizon.
Fish and crane
Swam through the white bowl of blue air,
Spinning outward upon
Mountainous heights and their soft mysterious pulleys.

My naked shoulders ached for the tumbling clouds,
And my shivering legs
Thrashed through those mossy fishing meadows,
Over the rose-pebbled bottoms,
And churned in the chilled and iridescent spawn
Of the crane's pool.
Clamped and flexed in the vise of her beating wings
Now flaring astride the brassy eye of the sun,
I gasped like a fish
Hung out in the harsh and sudden air
And flipped, past sparkling regions, underground.

Sacrifice of the Sparrows of the Field

My mother and sisters washed out each other's
Hair in sweet lemons and purest rainwaters;
And so did the neighboring girls and their mothers,
Lounging on porchswings on long summer mornings.
      Whenever the rain fell
      They ran with pails full
      Of water from eavespouts
      Pouring in cisterns.
When I dribbled a milkwhitened pebble downward
Into the softwater well depth, it whispered
In circles of girlfaces, wreathed and laughing;
Maybe it didn't, and maybe it mattered.
      But sparrows clogging
      The eavetroughs hanging
      Under our houses
      Were clouding our waters.
Horse hair and barn straw and cow dung together
They wove into cozy egg homes as they twittered,
And downy cock feathers in scissor-beaks shredded,
With mosses and mudroots packed in for filler.
      Dark summer showers
      And spouting baubles
      Broke from our shingles
      On sisters and mothers.
Whenever straight hair hung stringy and oily
My father and brothers were cursing the sparrows,
And up in the rain went the twin-sliding ladders,
And down came the baby sparrows, splashing.
      Naked wet sorrows,
      Babes in my palms, then,
      Bled out of tenderness.
      Dying becalmed them.
God knew that they clogged the troughs with odd odors
And, filthy with lice from their barnridden feathers,

Strained to our wells. Then sisters' and mothers'
Hair hung unwashed on their breasts and their shoulders.
        For whatever is hanging—
        Angel or evil—
        Over our eyelids,
        God must be answering.
In a crown of sweet Sundays, their services psalming
In wreaths of hair-presses and redolent showers,
Golden and brown under summerlace bonnets,
The rainwater mothers and sisters are singing
        Bird-warbled summer
        And rain-washed dripping
        In cisterns drumming.
        Bless the sweet sinner,
But our fine rural ladies must wash in rainwater.
We climb in our world, all brothers and fathers,
And run where it bells us, attacking and loving,
To sing the pure Sunday of sisters and mothers.

And sleep out the years in the arms of our lovers.

Song at Evening

Alone, the evening falls on me
along the cloud-swept day;
I walk the dusty roadway with
the soft feet of rain.

If you, beside your lonely bed,
say for me one prayer
I would not care if anyone
knows all my tears.

I stood beside the edge of town
and tried a broken tune;
if you should hear that wayward song
tell me, you'll come.

I saw a flower hanging low
by a still blue pond,
and as the rain and sun came down
it opened. That was all.

My Own Country

for Joey, Buffie, and Paul

At home in my own country
riding three horses   bareback into the morning,
    jogging out under the early blue
patched skies   with a vague white
      mist in the valleys,

    we hear the breathing
silence. Dew   hangs in tall grasses.
    On the ridge past Bekkan's Barn
sunlight is sifting   gradually through
      oaks and cottonwoods.

    Under our bodies
the trim hooves   of one brown and two
    matched dapple-gray horses clop
and muffle the dust.   Our leather bridle reins
      lie on their lean necks.

    A frightened
speckled grouse,   scattering the quackgrass,
    churns upward into a ragged flock
of chittering sparrows.   A few late chills
      shiver the edge

    of the barley fields.
On the next hill   Thor Flatberg's chimney
    puffs with a wisp of wood-smoke.
We turn and smile,   softly bouncing
      on Jupiter, May and June.

    He rears and whinnies,
shaking his sloppy bit;   May snickers and
    chuckles with her blubbery mouth;
June, prancing sideways,   suddenly farts
      and kicks her heels.

        We roll and rise
easily and slowly   upon their silken backs.
        Our faces lift to the long light
over the eastern woods;   our sinewy thighs
        are warmly filled

        until time stops.
You didn't ask me   but I want to say
        we all, yes, all of us, love
her who rides   beside us, and him
        who rides beside us,

        and the great mild beasts
nibbling the sharp air   with tough lips
        through the Folkedahl Meadows,
and grazing our legs   with warm flanks
        and flowing manes.

        We laugh. The horses
break into a hard trot   and then float off
        over the brief robes of morning
into a gallop, and   we are three swallows
        among the noisy sparrows.

Conversations from Childhood:
The Victrola

Lo, Here the Gentle Lark

When Alma Gluck
sang in high soprano,
  Lo,
Here the Gentle Lark,

on the scratched
ten-inch 78 record
to the old Victrola,

that little dog
was always listening
in the old horn.

Flutes sang, she sang—
larks singing together—
and he began.

And though time
goes terribly round
  & round
I am singing, still.

The Dog in the Horn

You dumb bloke,
you think steel needles
  can go
ten records without a mark?

Yeah, we watched
how the grooves got scored,
afraid the mended rota

would lose a cog.
We even tried group whistling
when the thing was gone.

Money went bang,
Depression came, dry weather,
no crops. Man!

Yessiree, I'm
looking for the tone
  and sound
of the world's goodwill.

Trilliums, Hepaticas, and Wood Lilies

Thinking of your light body half in water
where North Bear Creek and Rocky Spring together
meet in our bottomlands and valleys—
one from those Minnesota farms and town,
one from these Iowa hills—
thinking of that cool water,
your face half smiling from its surfaces,

seeing your brow above the watercress,
your hair against the quartz and granite stones
hung in the banks of green and tawny grass
where the moon fell fifty years ago,
I watch the sun
hang up its golden question to the sky.

I lift my hands to speak; suspended in themselves
they pause and start again,
letting my fingers memorize these riffles,
rising and dripping and falling,
the whole earth one long breath
of rippling substances.
Then the old willow and the great oaks and elms
put on the smallest breezes, their leaves turning
upon a cyclic pendulum of stems
blending over and over.
                        Seven shades of green
splash in a rainbow of wet eyelids
down half a century where those springlike waters
made for the open sea,
as though, once more, a bell
lifted its crystal lips where the two creeks ran together
and rang its silver tongue
around the sky-blue rim of the limestone cliff
while all the woodlands answered, wild with flowers.

Wood Pitch

I have been lovingly counting all this day long
Rock ferns and lilies in the limestone bluffs
And a few water cranes below.
Grown in them now
I think that the soul of this man,
His style, décor, fragrance, his present chains,
Are ferns and braided woodlilies and water cranes.

We are all, of course, circumscribed and chained
By the evanescent quality of our loves and fears
And are forever being defined
By statistical machines
Who think that the soul of man
Is only composite of all his furthest numbers
Plotted through daydreams and graphed among his slumbers.

I remember once, as a boy, reading the casual fact
That every seven years the cellular change
Of everyone's body is
Physically complete.
Am I not then sweet springs,
Air in a crane's wings, cool green in ferns,
And heat and light where the heart of the wood pitch burns?

You will say, won't you, that I evade the point,
That I translate all my percepts out of prose.
But who in the name of God
Ever, ever thought
That the ever-dancing soul,
Earthstoned, sunfired, haloed in airy mists,
Sleeps etherized for the young psychologists?

Sacrifice of the Dandelions

When all their gold blew up in a cloud
and threatened a silver blight on the land,
the entire neighborhood rose in arms
      and took a hand.

From April we labored to do them in,
ripping their tongues from the spongy lawn
and dumping their heads in velvet piles
      by the old trash bin.

In bags and buckets and wheelbarrow loads
we dug them out with knife and tine
and carted them off to the garbage stalls
      to wilt and die.

Though with the mower I trimmed the lawn
to an inch of its life, those flowers grew
flat on the turf till, plant by plant,
      we cut them through.

What pride and virtue, doing them in,
keeping our lawns entirely green,
graced by domestic flowers, sown
      as those had not been.

When the view from the porch was purely our own,
not a yellow head on the verdant sheen,
we gathered praises from houses and barns,
      being godly and clean.

Yet out in the pastures and barley fields
they gleamed in a thousand beds of gold,
and after a week rose up in a cloud—
      Oh, we all grow old—

and sailed into silvery mats on our lawns
and clung to our pure green grass like a snare
to give us our virtue another year
      and keep us right there.

The Soul Hears Its Country Childhood Singing Near the Edge of Town

First, the mother harp;
second, a fathering horn;
third a brother flute;
fourth, a sister bell;
fifth, the neighbor drum:
weeds, God, and a song.

How strange and natural was that song!
It gathered him in like a waterharp
plucked from the streams, a resident drum
booming with rain, like a father horn
in the rooms of God, like a sister bell
chiming the door to its brother flute.

Parables reared in the grass-whistle flute,
and pastures galloped on tufts of song
past Aprils of bleating snow in the bell.
Chickens scratched in the grain of the harp,
the bull exhaled in its hairy horn,
and the world went marketing off on a drum.

Church and barn and rain-barrel drum,
did an organ speak from a willow flute?
Or the touring Hudson's echoing horn
blare in a cellar and cave of song?
Or a hand in the upright piano harp
strike hymns and dust to a sunlit bell?

The afternoon sister ran with that bell
toward shadowy neighbors fenced in a drum;
then mother morning rose to the harp
and brother evening prayed with his flute
to the mocking darkness. Hard on that song
his high-noon father gilded his horn.

Hawk in the night and owl in the horn,
dove and sparrow and goldfinch bell,
are you God, or father, or sister song?
Grouse and red-headed woodpecker drum,
can you bless a jay with a cardinal flute?
Or meadowlark, nest in the mothering harp?

Rosewindow, fencewire, shine in your harp!
Peonies, boom in your velvet horn!
Crowfoot, bitter cup, harrow that flute!
Riot, anemone ferns, in that bell!
Time and religion, bloom in your drum!
And brother to neighbor, labor this song:

horn in the harp, and God in the horn,
flute in the weed, and bell in the song,
weeds and hours and years in the drum.

Ecclesiastes

Out of the icy storms the white hare came
Shivering into a haven of human arms;
It was not love but fear that made him tame.

He lay in the arms of love, having no name
But comfort to address. Shaking alarms
Out of the icy storms, the white hare came

Across the haunted meadows crackling with game.
What evil eye pinpointed his soft charms?
It was not love but fear. That made him tame

Among the chilling hail and scattering aim.
Helpless against the sport of ancient farms,
Out of the icy storms the white hare came

Thinking, perhaps, it leaped through icy flame,
Thinking, with instinct, hate or trust disarms.
It was not love. But fear that made him tame

Leaped again in his heart; his flesh became
Translated into havens. From sudden harms
Out of the icy storms the white hare came;
It was not love but fear that made him tame.

II

We felt another dream
rise in our flesh and feed
the mouth of mysteries.

The Wheel of Summer

The dark land rose in the luminous arch of sky.
The bald sun softly grew. Down by the barn
My father and we three sons watched how it fell
Through hazes of sour dust by the old pig pens.
"They got away from us," my father said.
He didn't need to say it. The great sun god
Bowed to the grassy sea by the western hills,
Darkened to blood, rolled in the tasseled corn
And flamed our blinking eyeballs. "Yup," we said,
And turned in the dirty twilight to our thoughts.

> Those silken shoats with jiggling nuts
> Went squealing under their mothers' tits
> Two months too long, until they ran
> Smelling each other around the pens
> And snuffled into a herd of lusts.
> Ourselves but fifteen, fourteen, twelve,
> We knew that wrestling those young boars
> And bearing them, sterile, up from the knives
> With bristling feet and foaming mouths
> Could bend our steel and twist our smiles.

We ambled, loose in overalls, up by the house.
We doused our barny hands in sun-warmed waters,
Waited for supper, glanced at the girls, then ate.
We counted a few odd stars and the evening star
Over the glut of summer. Later, upstairs,
We stripped and gathered a pillow into our arms,
Rolled in the humid nightfall once or twice,
Muttered a thing or two, then fell asleep.

> The women swept the kitchen,
> Carried the washing waters,
> Scrubbing towels and basins.
> We slept. They quietly chatted,
> Loosened their hair and spread it
> In puffs for summer dreaming.

Out of those dreaming coves
The dawn broke, suddenly,
And rolled the milk-dust haze
Up Bekkan's Ridge. We yawned,
Straightened the slack in our mouths,
Tightened our muscles a notch,
Wrinkled our groins like a gourd,
And marched on out to the barn.

Then Father called, "Let's drive them in."
We harried pigs toward the dusty barn,
Kicked the shoats and rammed the door
And banged the bar in its wooden home.
Coarse as our job, we whaled them all
Till some walked, upright, on the gates
And flowed together. "Wet them down!"
In the stock-tank our buckets swam,
Slipped and swished and, bellying up,
Went shivering over the slithering pens.
Our badgered strength was out of mind
In summer madness: a sty of sounds.

Our father, priest and teacher, led us on.
We stood in the sire's circle while he talked,
Whipped out his knife and whetted it on stone.
He flipped some acrid Lysol from his jug
To test it out, then touched the slicing blade
Gingerly over his thumb. All set to go.
"Boys, let's bring them on." We'd bring them on.

We eyed the mob,
Curious, queasy.
Gray dust flowered
Under the rafters.
Breathy and muddy,
They surged together
In sour odors.

The three of us dove down the herd.
I grabbed one, dared not let him go.
Some boyish pride threw out my arms
To catch the unsuspecting world.
They clamped like iron. Crushing him,
I locked him to my chest and bore
Him, staggering, to the trough. Hair,
Plastered with dust, bristled my arms.
"Hup, flip him now!" Damned if I didn't,
But square on his feet. Off he ran,

His bony tail stretched outward from my hands,
He charged the herd. I hauled him down again,
And up from the pigsty floor we two arose,
Loudly embracing. And for what purposes?
"Hang on this time!" You think I would've lost him?
I knew when we were working, not at games,
When to be gentle, when to play it rough;
One cannot breed ten thousand animals
Into this world and woo them for the axe
Without a curse and prayer to help him through.

I got him upside down in the trough
And hung on his heels. I stomped his chest.
My brother locked his squealing snout.
With Lysol, tender flesh was doused;
That knife dipped in the slickest stroke
I ever saw this side of hell,
And murderous music, like a crime,
Gurgled that milk-blue blooded dream.

Snip went the cords; the mindless body doubled.
Flick went the blade again; the shades of change
Rolled down the dust beyond the feeding troughs,
A tough abstraction. Dropping the crippled pig,
We rolled him out and ran him down the alley.
He walked so gingerly he seemed to dance

With quivering hooves upon the ragged straw
Along the barn. The solemn way he went,
He must have dumbly felt some ancient law
Driving him out of nature's benediction.

> Infected with truth,
> We hung in dust
> Drenched to our skins,
> Bleached to our bones.
> He sat in the straw
> Mute as a rock,
> Crudely undone.
> Ranker than swine,
> Coarse to our nails
> We swung to our job.

> Then we went all the way
> To common terms with loss.

> Having run down our guilt and pain,
> We lobbed the curses from our mouths.

We trapped them all. We never bore so much
Next to our hearts. We caught them with our feet,
Caged them for death and shrilled them back to life
To trot, untroubled, fattening for your grace.
So we prepared your table. The awful world
Seemed natural as breathing. Brazen with swine,
We hounded the living daylights out of the earth.
Nature we rolled, denatured, in the straw
Where loss waits in the alleys like a snake,
Coiled and ready, although it cannot strike.
The last lay down exhausted, wouldn't run.
We could have lain down with him. Had he fought
We might have, in our weakness, let him go.
At last, we spun the gates and turned them out
Under the bur oak trees by the young alfalfa.
The barrows wandered through the blooming grasses.
We poured some water for their healing mudbaths.

We filled their troughs with generous sour mashes.
Burying snouts, they snuffled in rows of pigs' eyes,
And we, stinking high heaven, turned and trotted
Slowly along the woodpaths into the valley.

How shall I praise the valley waters,
The crystal springs so sweetly aching
Over our bruised, our lusty bodies?

We slid in water like sluggish wishes
And lay on sandbanks, mute and weary.
The water idled over our heartbeats.

We blew cool water out of our noses
With the clotted curses and gray mucus
And rose in our summer limbs for drying.

From sparkling stones we walked; then, dressing
In cleanest clothes on the polished gravels,
We stretched ourselves on yielding grasses,

While healing evening came.
We felt another dream
Rise in our flesh and feed
The mouth of mysteries;
It flickered in our minds
And quivered in our thighs.
Sweeping across our limbs,
It loosed our fumbling tongues
Until, at last, we talked
About the neighbor girls
And joked among ourselves.

We rose from the banks. For the evening star
Our casual wishes and shadowy groves
Welled with a tougher grace. To the barn
We rocked with the great maternal cows
And milked them down with our gentlest hands.

Next morning took us like an old surprise.
Fallen, with old corruption in our arms,
We praised the animal urgencies of love,
Our long obedience. The mind of man,
Boyishly wandering out of the eye of God,
Seemed natural to our wills. Our bruised bones
Took on this sweet admission. Proud in the sun,
Calloused and cocked, wicked and wise and young,
We ran, three golden idols, back to chores,
Shouldered the wheel of summer, and journeyed on.

III

A green weather of boughs
tells us to search for heaven out of this,
and the top limbs let us down.

A Little Homily
for the Holy Seasons of the Spirit

for Rachel Carson

Through all my childhood I
Often beheld ragged sparrows
Flying upward throughout a series of lesser fallings,
Beating their filmy feathers against the nest-clogged barn
           eaves.
Being no St. Francis feeding
Among the field lilies,

I fell through tumbling air.
It is scarcely daring for birds
To begin falling; then grace is natural. Bedazzling
Flight begins in descent until lovelier upswinging
Embraces the side-slipping wings.
Then birds fly and heart skips.

Descent is good folly;
Therefore, it is sometimes holy
Inasmuch as bird-natural worlds are an expression,
In ranges of goodness and omnipresent wickedness,
Of bright platonic otherworlds
And omnipotent wills.

Think how young hummingbirds
Flutter out from motherworld homes
While birdsmall bones, immaculately curving and hollowed,
Find that the air is home and all flight hallowed orisons.
History makes orioles, doves,
Swallows saintly. And gulls,

Though sung briefly. Gaze by
The twirling life-span of God's birds.
One sees them battered by windshields of your bishop's Buick,
Pounced on by amoral cats, shocked by boy-triggered rifles,
Frozen through hungers unto death,
Poisoned for plagues of filth

In the human cities.
Oh, from any open window
Bede's sad and fleeting sparrow, Shelleyan larks, the rough ark's
Dove, the militant eagle, penguins of Anatole France
Flee past spiritual atolls
Of a priori soul

Into birdlike islands.
Though divine illusion insists
That natural flight is holiness, it is no such thing;
We ascend to destruction and fall to the realms of grace.
But if all birds fell from the air
Imagine our despair.

Imagine orioles
Spinning their orange flames toward earth,
Millions of barn swallows not rising out of their dipping,
Odd birds of paradise falling out of their paradise
Heavy as stones and dipped arrows,
And hosts of dead sparrows.

Imagine all soaring
Fieldlarks now silently falling,
Even the parrots and guinea hens ceasing their squawking,
Water ouzels not singing, every bald eagle fallen,
Sandpipers and rosy grossbeaks,
Shrikes, canaries and teals

All falling. Imagine
These feathery constellations
Tumbling on snow peaks, on green plains and turquoise sea
                    waters,
Cardinals, goldfinches, wrens, bluebirds falling from graces,
These rainbowing appellations
All falling. Imagine!

And silently falling!
Even the raucous crows, alas,
And saw-winged buzzards silent, magpies, camp-robbers,
                    blue jays,

Bobwhites, owls, nuthatches, blackbirds! How would you
          like to see
The mourning dove making no moan
And the phoenix a stone?

And all the gulls plunging
Down into waves forevermore
In deathly congregations? And bright mothlike
          hummingbirds
Crushed in Canterbury chalices? The olive-white dove,
Despite all heaven's commotions,
Lost in endless oceans?

Oh, it is neither good
Nor evil that troubles us here,
But rather spiritual affinities. I have now
Spoken of ascension, resurrection and death. In you
They all lodge in disguises of
Holy and profane love.

Singing in Late Summer

Singing at the piano, in late summer,
a Nordic folksong, *Den Store Hvide Flok,*
by the two windows
in the northwest corner of our living room
with one blue with late light over the western hills
and the other wide on the deep thicket of evening,
here in my home in western Massachusetts,

and my father ten years dead
and my mother eighty years old a thousand miles away
and slowly growing older,
and my eight brothers and sisters, blood of my heart,
scattered dead and alive over the face of the earth,
and my wife absent a while from these rooms she made,
and my children lately gone,

I feel the hollows under the shadowy woods
moistly expand and move,
gathering the strange authority of darkness
and breathing and seeping and creeping under the sills
until the flipping pages of my mind
wave like ghosts in the windowpane
and turn my booming song of the Great White Host
back to that black and tremulous silence
from which, I suppose, it came.

The Cobra

The hooded cobra floating over the leaves
Indescribably deceives,
Flicking his delicate forked tongue in rings
By blasted mosses where his body swings
In powerful convolutions. The scaly scarp
Of his flat diamond head forswears his sharp
Flickering pointed eyes
Relaying all surprise
Through coiling coils to his mouth's elastic sheath
Tissued over his venomed teeth.

Yet in the sleep that followed after fear
I saw the sheer
Sharp curves and striking shape resolved
Toward light, the nest of coils dissolved
Into a birdlike body; that proud head thrust
Rose to its kingly grace from bleaching dust;
White feathers crept
Along the elongated neck, then swept
Downily over the changing eyes. I saw dust break
Into a dew, and then a lake,
And where the dark tormentor once had gone
Rode a triumphant swan.

War

When my young brother was killed
By a mute and dusty shell in the thorny brush
Crowning the boulders of the Villa Verde Trail
On the island of Luzon,

I laid my whole dry body down,
Dropping my face like a stone in a green park
On the east banks of the Rhine;

On an airstrip skirting the Seine
His sergeant brother sat like a stick in his barracks
While cracks of fading sunlight
Caged the dusty air;

In the rocky rolling hills west of the Mississippi
His father and mother sat in a simple Norwegian parlor
With a photograph smiling between them on the table
And their hands fallen into their laps
Like sticks and dust;

And still other brothers and sisters,
Linking their arms together,
Walked down the dusty road where once he ran
And into the deep green valley
To sit on the stony banks of the stream he loved
And let the murmuring waters
Wash over their blood-hot feet with a springing crown
                of tears.

A Love for God

The sudden rocky rooms at waterfalls
        Contain us as we climb.
            They batter down
Our earthly aspirations, while our hearts
Leap to that haven where the water springs,
        The cool draughts of love.

Washing with endless waters all our limbs,
        Sea, in its paler mask,
            Entices us.
We sink to it; it whitens in our hair.
Fall and be loved completely while you can,
        Then rise, or slowly drown.

Even the shades of trees invite us up
        Into a breeze of loves.
            That cave of leaves
Hides us from friends. A green weather of boughs
Tells us to search for heaven out of this,
        And the top limbs let us down.

Shall we assault the mountains? There they stand
        Coldly awaiting us.
            We go to them.
Over luxuriant foothills body runs
Until it flees the snow in hostile heights,
        Shakes once, and shivers down.

God always threatens. His love makes us bold.
        It is almost too much
            To touch your hands,
Extremities that fall and freeze and drown.
But though an insanity of happiness is death,
        I'll go. And then come home.
            Our peace will come.

A Sea-Change: For Harold

Across the swamps and marshlands of the hours,
Over the cloud-banked air and under the dark
Hills of fog where lamps
Float incandescent caves in drowsy streets,
The drowned sound of the sea wells up in foghorns
Blowing out of their watery towns.
That chilled gray groan
Rises on sunken mountains, upon
Oceanic rain-eroded shores, under
Hollow crystal gongs in icy poles,
And rides through cabled water-years of sound
To echo upward over the rusty buoys,
Bobbing and clanging in a blind mist
Along our inward bays,
To cry an old sad song in the soggy bones
Under our chalky shores.

The cold ache and dull blue sound of the sea
Fades in the foaming crests,
Whispers at rocks
Jutting their gray-green heads from the gray-green sea,
And sleeps in the world's great valleys.
There the riding ocean sighs
Over the shoals of continental shelves
Down to submerged kingdoms
Where drowned soldiers, logged in the sound,
Dream that their salt-encrusted eyes
Glow in the weeds and corals of their skulls.

Across broad rivered deltas and crumbling cliffs
That long gray sound
Faintly vibrates over the ocean floor
And rises under our surface solitudes
As if a huge volcano, muffled under the sea,
Erupted with no sound.

Buchenwald, Near Weimar

Through barbed-wire enclosures,
Their bodies bloodless under metallic thorns
    Like an unauthorized crucifixion,
The animal faces of handsome Europe steered
    And grinned and begged and leered.

They had piled some bodies up,
Naked to God, like cordwood for a fire.
    If eyes and faces turned,
Or jaws hung out among the shriveled limbs,
    They sang, thank God, no hymns.

Pallid with black dishonor,
Nailed to the numerals of striped uniforms,
    Stripped of their native hair,
They snared me with their unashamed display
    And mocked at my dismay.

A rapid frantic babbling
I took for a Slavic tongue, a complete stranger,
    But a wrinkled skeleton
Wavered up the wire and whispered in English,
    His mind is sick. In anguish

The proud white brow of man,
Where the eye nobly shines, had crashed down.
    It groveled on the ground,
More than Greece falling, more than Rome
    Razed in its charred home.

The low gray barracks stood
Dumb, in a chained line, in the torn-up land.
    The bleak doggy eyes

Rolled to and fro, compounded with despair,
    Blind to the exit there.

        I could not touch them; I could
Not ask forgiveness, not even comfort them.
        I came from another land
And stood at the deathbed of my own father again
In that vast mad graveyard of falling men.

The Lotus Flower

In 1840, the year of his marriage to Clara, Robert Schumann
wrote 138 songs, of which "The Lotus Flower" is one.

Now it is one hundred and thirty-six years later.
For almost a month now,
from the 14th of June to the 4th of July,
I have been trying to sing "The Lotus Flower" by Schumann
to an English text adapted from Heinrich Heine.
The days burn toward the sun;
the flower turns toward the moon.

Through oaks and maples at my eastern windows
clear radiance flows down upon my house.
This sun, at its generous distance,
marries the elements and warms me.
Last night
I even thought I saw it smiling in the full face of the moon.
I, too, might blossom there,
as I think I almost do
in this song, in this room, in these strings,
under the arch of these boughs,

but

thirty-one years ago
I stood in my infantry soldier's uniform
puzzling out the elaborate German Gothic lettering
of some lines from Heinrich Heine—
"Let not disgusting worms consume my body;
give me the clear bright flame"—
done on parchment in an oaken frame
over the concrete arch
of the door to the crematorium
at Buchenwald, nach Weimar,
where three brick ovens
fed their red hearts to the sun.

My hands, in the six-four time, keep faltering
heavily over the black and white keys
and I hear my voice saying, "The lotus flower
lies drooping
under the sun's warm light,"
over those huge repeated modulating chords.

I sit in the mottled sunlight of my home
more than four thousand miles away,
alone in another hemisphere.
As the chords change
my foot lifts and falls on the left steel pedal,
dampening the discords.

Again my hands pause; my foot wanders, waits.
So as not to stumble,
I lift it carefully over the concrete doorsill.
My voice begins to fail. The sun
glows on the low barracks. Through the square door
the light shifts
in the green leaves and sifts
over our white faces
like ashes.

I close the piano; I put my book away
and head for the outside door,
sunlit and gray.

Rock

Observed from age to age,
The water's arrogance
Stabs at the earth, a rage
Of damned munificence.

Spun from the ocean plains
Clear to its polar caps,
Who knows what world it drains,
What country takes? Perhaps

It lures and smiles and lies
Beyond our sandy sweeps;
Yet, seen with ageless eyes,
Whole armies from its deeps

Rise on our shores and crash
Over our walls. One hears
Only that single clash
Joined for a million years.

If patience were a rock,
Anger the pounding sea,
I should prefer to mock
That mad intensity;

And though I, grain by grain,
Fail in those fluid wars,
I still might entertain
Such thundering visitors

As long as one could shout.
As far as one could hear,
Until the earth give out
Or judgment reappear.

A Hiroshima Lullaby

For Sadako Sasaki, dead of leukemia in October 1955, at the age of
twelve. A few months before her death she tried to fold 1,000 paper
cranes which, according to Japanese legend, would protect her health.
She had reached 964 when she died. Her childhood classmates
completed the magic thousand and raised money for her statue,
holding a golden crane, in the Peace Park in Hiroshima.

Sadako, you have gone
beyond the fire's fear;
we follow where you walk
upon that magic hill.

The Hiroshima birds
come back across the sea
into the city square.
Sleep now, Sadako, sleep.

Now on the darkest nights
the shadows on the waves
lift from your fallen eyes
upon a cloud of cranes.

They march across the sky,
a thousand in a line
to keep their watch upon
the children in their dreams.

Sadako, here's a star
to cradle in your hand
and fly around the sun
and nest upon the moon.

Sadako, paper girl,
ride on your thousand wings
and cry your gentle prayer.
We fold your paper cranes.

A Stone for a Maker

Rolfe Humphries, 1894–1969

Brought to this old translation of ourselves,
   imagining truth to the source,
we lie in a mask of memory under the quick
   eyelids of our world.
                I woke, he almost said,
                to the thought of music.
A playful light, transparent, folds and lifts,
   turns in a shadow, smiles
in crafty undulations, then gathers in
   word upon phrase on line.
                Three sirens sat in the barley,
                fluting upon a straw.
Once, in a greener country, David went
   humming through hedge and farm,
ragged among the brambles. He taught his tongue
   the grace of a strong harp;
                Even the daylight, itself,
                practiced upon his fingers.
he made it shake the heavy weeds with love
   and riffle the village streams,
while flocks of flittering sparrows broke the clumps
   of thistles into a sweet
                (How sweet that music was,
                the song that silences)
suspended audience. Listen to the measure
   vibrating the very airs
of the strung throat of the hoarse singer still
   twanging among the heralds.
                Beating a stick on a stump
                is almost enough for a drum.
Hunger, he sang, and hollow absence flung
   over the rocky halls,
and soiled mantles, drifting upon the wind,
   and love, a broken psalm.
                It's what we mend that makes
                us menders of anything.

And mercy, whoever he is, he cried for him,
        that white and tardy fool
running the seas and hills. How shall we keep
        justice snug in our rooms?
                        There are many answers, too.
                        Try one, he said, on me.
Or green armor on green ground? Or the cunning
        harp in broken hands?
Or bend the words to the song, making them do
        what the poem understands?
                        Everything comprehends
                        itself in becoming itself.
So rags for the body, sing, and a cup of beer,
        and sing the ruddy fire,
and a few companions to pluck away the nights
        from the battering bell of time.
                        And if time does not ring
                        he'll clap it to, again.
Then let the vasty spirits of the cliffs
        rage on the vales and coves
and run the greenest valley underground,
        loving the dumb stones.

A Little Day-Music for My Departed Sister

Corrine, wake up!   the dog's at the door,
truck in the yard,   dust on the floor,
flies on the screen;   the swinging clock
is the day's chores   and the heart's knock.

That deep sigh   for all that has been
is only a whisper   of an old pain
that is dying away   in memory, green
as a fair life   and a good name.

The blue skies   are tilled and plowed,
filled up with sun,   pulled down with cloud.
Friends and neighbors,   fancy and plain,
do what you know,   see what you've seen.

Nothing the earth   can yield to us
is more than your shovel   uplifting a rose,
more than your kitchen   flooded with light,
bright in the morning,   dark in the night.

Corrine, wake up!   All we have known
of wheat kernels   and heart stones
is little beside   the proud blood
that carried your head   in our neighborhood.

The graveled roads   run up and down;
friends still walk   in Decorah, Waukon;
and the days rise,   brown white black green
among your heartiest   loves, Corrine.

Corrine, wake up!   and greet the morn.
Your rose by the kitchen   is fragrant, the thorn
is polished with dew   and the sweet alarm
of the sun invading   the underground.

Now even the root   of death is calm,
and the far night   and northwest storm.
And we are abroad   in earth and flame
to call from the air   once more, your name.

Corrine, wake up!   dogs at the door,
trucks in the yard,   dust on the floor.
Too much to do   before you lie down,
or put on your dress   and ride into town.

Too much to think of,   rain, wind, and sun,
the house untidy,   the days undone
night after night   and dawn after dawn.
God only knows   where you might have gone.

Holding Them Still

When we are up and about, all sleep seems
a starlit silence, as though the soul might well
forget a third of its days, breathy with dreams.

Yet sometimes, in early autumn, we get
all along the western horizon for an hour
just after the sun has set,

especially when country and town
have been without any rain for a little while,
the graces of earth in a blue crown

entirely luminous and clear.
Yes, in such a tremulous hour we get
the sense of far things being near.

Why, we can see for miles everywhere.
There is nothing that seems either too far away
or yet too near. Look there!

at that tree way off, and this easily seen
bur oak tree that is standing beside us here—
both the same posture of darkening green.

And even though one is larger and nearer
it would not seem right for anyone to claim
that either is sharper or clearer.

Perhaps such prefigurations can trail
our winking and blinking on retina and nerve,
like faith upon hope until we fail

and our bodies merely serve
as an ancient school of memory; earth and sky
fade in their spaces as into a curve

of sparkling darkness. Try
as we may we cannot, simply cannot, hold them still.
They grace, moment by moment, the severe eye,

outdistancing ourselves. They darken our will.
See! they are going: these hands, this tree there,
our road, those upland fields, that further hill,

while sun and sky, the parasitical green,
subside in muffled shadows, sheen on sheen,
and glow in the dust and dew, unseen,

like Karen, Clara Elizabeth, and Corrine.

Windflower Songs: For Harvey Swados

He loved the olives of Southern France and the maples here, Brooklyn
Heights and the Village and Washington Mews, the Berkshires and
Chesterfield Gorge, his flute and the piano and harp, Mozart and
Beethoven and Mahler, Stendhal and the memoirs of Herzen,
anemones, cardinals, airedale dogs, yes, and the color blue.
—Bette Swados

The olive and the maple stand,
a southern slope, a northern land,
and take by local presence there
a range of color from the air.

For leaf, one makes a duller green:
the maple brighter, shade and sheen.
One maintains it to the end;
the other flames and comes again.

For sky, one asks a softer blue,
Mediterranean in its hue;
the other likes it sharp and bold:
blue that blazes, blue that's cold.

And both are harps that in them tell
insects and parasites, as well;
the old dove from the olive calls,
from maple, whistling cardinals.

For structure, one is twisted, spread;
the other towers overhead.
One, sun and shadow interlaid,
the other, deep in summer shade.

One likes the Berkshires for a stance;
the other, all of Southern France.
They bless our villages and prove
as graceful in a country grove.

Take your Stendhal and your dog;
sit down against a maple log,
and page through one provincial town
while Julian brings the olives down.

Then read by shovel, pick and hoe,
by shrill assemblies, row by row,
a raging fist of words. Then shout.
And love? It simply knocked him out.

The maple's juice is sugar-sweet,
the olive bitter. When we eat,
as when we talk, the mind is stung
by such a balance on the tongue.

Carve maple, olive, flute by flute,
they keep the hardness of their root,
and hold such grains before our eyes
as took an age to compromise.

That tough discretion grows and clears
the humors of a hundred years.
God, bring an olive from the South
and hard rock maple from the North.

No matter where they stood, or are,
their nature is their metaphor:
a celebration, known at last
by overflowing, standing fast.

Dry Grass

The hayfield whispers as I walk
Each midnight hour up this hill
To tell the autumn wind such talk
And nonsense as I will.
I mark the sumac by the moon
And tear the withered grass to show
How crisp stems crackle, and how soon
The searching fingers know
Beyond old callouses and tough
Thin tentacles of nerve that this
Is death again.

              I like that rough
Sharp certainty that is
Portion of hand and part of mind.
For if, sometimes, I run in fear,
Bewildered, questioning and blind,
At least I have death here,
Real in my human hand. It
Is reassuring, being clean
And common to my autumn wit
And in my memory, green.

Ballad of Poor Will

I was got with a cowlick, and so will I end,
    Sunlight and summer and sun,
My hair all awry, even into the grave,
                Into the grave,
And even there twisting. God, may you send,
    Starlight and autumn and rain,
Grimaces and psalmings to mull in my face,
    Washing and making me clean.

Burn all my blemishes, scattered and splotched,
    Sunlight and summer and sun;
They even unbalanced the wings of my brain,
                Wings of my brain.
If dust will accept them, wrinkled and botched,
    Starlight and autumn and rain,
It can slowly reject them. Let the years fail,
    Washing and making me clean.

For I had a birthmark, and I had a love,
    Sunlight and summer and sun,
One harsh on my neck and one soft in my arms,
                Soft in my arms,
One cold in my heart and one deep in the grove,
    Starlight and autumn and rain,
But I cherished the chill, and I wasted the warmth
    Washing and making me clean.

And I got a scar on my strong right thigh,
    Sunlight and summer and sun,
And a wart on my hand, some moles on my back,
                Moles on my back,
And a wandering vein in the edge of my eye,
    Starlight and autumn and rain . . .
Oh, take me again to the old mummy sack,
    Washing and making me clean.

Dear God, be more wary of all that you send,
    Sunlight and summer and sun,
All stumbling and beating and twitching alive,
                        Twitching alive,
For it takes forever, you know, just to mend,
    Starlight and autumn and rain,
The self for the self, with never a wife
    Washing and making me clean.

All errors accepting, you let me be born,
    Sunlight and summer and sun.
How long till it end! It is troublesome hard,
                    Troublesome hard,
To thread the dark thickets of neighboring scorn,
    Starlight and autumn and rain,
With only a prayer for the blackest reward
    Washing and making me clean.

When I'm five years under then dig in my ground,
    Sunlight and summer and sun,
And tenderly scrape me all off in the wind,
                    Off in the wind,
Then put me all back, for my bones are sound,
    Starlight and autumn and rain,
With a ghost of a blessing to you from Poor Will.
    Washing and making me clean.

Schweitzer

When Albert Schweitzer plays Johann Sebastian Bach
On his zinc-lined organ in Equatorial Africa,
The jungle evening cries in a carol of birds.
    (When the heart's eye is true
    Spirit will worship you.)
His healing fingers announce the preludes and fugues,
And broken arpeggios ring; then birds respond
In miniature oratorios, while their black throats
    (Obscenities they learned
    In the wild garden, spurned)
Shake the bright chain of echoes over their homes.
They come from broad-bladed palms, where primitive
          shades
Sleep and brood in their wings and rainbowing plumes
    (Aisles they, feinting, run
    Teaching them into the sun),
And sing, being ignorant, the only songs they know:
Flights of chaconnes, masses, and passacaglias
Wheezing from pumping bellows to whistling mouths
    (That swooping passion grown
    Toward pilgrimaging tone).
Hearing praise, they praise by instinct. Crown on crown
Of improbable song wheels over their music master;
They mimic all keys in a chaos of shrill chorales.
    (Antiphonal with games,
    Their organs pipe his names.)
It is evening, the birds at their mass. The pagan sky
In a rose of paradise gathers its feathered saints,
Vibrating their tiny flutes in thousands of throats
    (Redeemed in the simple bliss
    Of innocent artifice),
Skillfully chanting. Deep in that day-breeding dusk,
Oh, when this man is dead, let us say that he taught
The unwieldiest birds of the jungle the music of Bach
    (Making man imagine men's
    Pride in their sad amens),
Where, wide on the rim of this world, we mask that face
Fugue-flying, patiently following, putting in place
The darkening souls of earth with amazing grace.

Winter Juniper

Above these bleak Wyoming plains,
These high plateaus
Where water seldom rises through the rock,
This twisting cedar grows.
Splitting through sharp and sandy grains
Of buried cliffs, its fragrant seedlings mock
Deep humus soils and rains.

Under a bright December sun
This cedar pricks
With waxed and polished stems the arid air,
Pivots angular sticks,
Quivers in western winds; they run
Through and away. Here with such final care
Its tortured life is done,

And done, and done again, until
The grained wood
Spirals into a balance, a defense,
A grace. One night I stood
Under the moon in a midnight chill,
Caught in that alien axis, grown immense
In that green will.

IV

And I'm not surprised seeing
some people at morning
crying, "God a mercy!"

Sacrifice of a Rainbow Trout

Suddenly, from the rocky spring
A trout hung, trembling, in the air,
A jewel to the morning sun;

And then upon the mossy banks,
Rainy with rainbows, up he leaped
And tumbled wildly in the grass.

I ran to catch him where my hook
Pinned him behind a crusted rock
And ripped his mouth and gills apart.

I pulled his foaming stomach clean
And washed my fingers in the spring
And sat down and admired him.

His sunlit scales upon my hands,
I wrapped his flesh in leaves of elm
And homeward, singing, carried him.

I stripped him of his ivory bones,
Then held him, shining, to the fire
And tongued his body to my own.

And that was the supper that I had
While my imagination fed
Its silver hook upon the world.

Sacrifice of Gophers and Woodchucks

When I was a young one
I used to trap gophers
(10¢ for the ears, and 15¢ for the hide)
And caught woodchucks.
It was all business pride;
Nobody stung one.

I got up at five—
I mean, really early—
(10¢ for the ears, and 15¢ for the hide)
And jangled my traps
At my shoulder sides;
Man, I was alive.

I carried a stick-club
In my right hand, always
(10¢ for the ears, and 15¢ for the hide).
It was all you needed
To finish them off with:
A quick sharp thud.

Gophers brought thistles.
That's what neighbors said
(10¢ for the ears, and 15¢ for the hide).
They ruined the grainfields,
The whole countryside.
Had sharp whistles.

Pa didn't like them.
Neither did I
(10¢ for the ears, and 15¢ for the hide).
If he had a pitchfork
By when I caught one,
Quick, he'd spike him.

When taut chains drag
In a woodchuck's hole
(10¢ for the ears, and 15¢ for the hide),
You know, if it goes
All slack on the guide,
She bit off a leg.

Easy, I pulled them
Home from their burrows
(10¢ for the ears, and 15¢ for the hide);
Then's when I slugged them.
It saved my pride
For when I sold them.

Inflation caught me
By my confirmation
(10¢ for the ears, and 15¢ for the hide).
It seems that I never
Will keep my pride
With what that brought me.

But I like looking back
On those natural hours
(10¢ for the ears, and 15¢ for the hide),
Barefoot at dawn
With chucks on the hills,
Fresh ears in my sack.

This is not hearsay.
I've been a young trapper
(10¢ for the ears, and 15¢ for the hide),
And I'm not surprised seeing
Some people at morning
Crying, "God a mercy!"

Sacrifice of the Golden Owl

We strung our Wyandotte rooster, dead, on a post
And wired him fast, head up, white wings outspread
Just under the woodchuck trap. Then went to bed.

All night those great jaws looking at the sky
Above the swollen eyeballs of our cock
Waited for morning. But nothing made them lock.

Whatever it was that fed upon our world
Delayed his visiting, or else mistook
Those puffed red wattles with too close a look.

We thought it was some talon out of heaven,
Some claw-hook of the sky, some steel-hooked beak
With which we hoped our woodchuck trap would speak.

At last it did. Diving at striking noon,
A golden owl spilled downward like a sun,
Split my blue sky, and with the trap was one.

The feathered chain sang out and jerked until
I whacked his twisting head against that post.
He flopped, then ebbed, and dangled with his ghost.

I took him to the woodshed, sprang my knife,
And slit the shining golden breast apart,
Only to find a miserably small heart.

Then father cried, "Go take the rooster down."
I burned him with the trash, then ran and stood
The owl's heart on my new-split kindling wood.

I made a little ritual of that fire
To warm my heart, but wept above that breath
Singeing the tough cold bitterness of death,

And choked on the foulest odors of his wings
While all that dazzling plumage fanned upon
The plundered underworld which we had won.

Sacrifice of a Gunnysack of Cats

The quick small bubbles popping from the gunnysack,
Hooked by a pitchfork braced in the cattle tank,
Almost unhinged my heart and made me drop
The stick with which I forced the young cats down.

A population explosion, that's what it was.
With twelve mother cats and a year of visiting toms
We met September with the wildest host
Of squinting eyes behind our milking cows.

We divvied them up among the brothers and sisters,
And each had only six. But since we were nine
My father thought things were getting out of hand.
Next day I received my melancholy orders.

"You'll have to catch the most of them and drown them.
Just tidy up the place and make it normal.
Fifty-four cats! Why, that's an infernal nuisance.
Think what would happen next year!" What could I tell him?

So there I was dashing with my gunnysack
Into the bins and under the stalls and mangers.
The wild ones scratched me, but I thrust them in.
The tame ones? Oh, I brushed them with my cheek,

Sighed and kissed them, then I thrust them in.
I climbed the ladders to the highest mows,
Ran through the orchard under the heavy apples
And crept among the tall weeds by the granary,

Until I thought I could not bear that cross.
I dropped it once; that made it twice as hard
To lure them once again into that womb
And bear it backward to the spermal waters.

But there I was: filthy, bleeding, and sick,
Tired and thirsty, my cord pulled at its neck,
The undulating coffin on my waggon,
Trudging down to the sea, my cross upon me.

The thorny dissonance of dying song
Over the squealing of the wagon wheels
Ran up a cloud of dust that nearly drowned me.
It is one thing to think, and one to do.

I wanted to avoid the thinking in the doing
And, quick, be done with it and off to play.
But you can see this didn't work too well . . .
Thirty-three years to get that cord untied.

I stood in the dust manure at my feet,
The green scum in the corners of the tank
Eyeing my smothering conscience toward a size
My body could not hold. Good God, I seized

That squirming sepulchre, that crying tomb,
That leaping heart familiar as myself,
And heaved it from my homemade hearse and plunged
It back to evolution. Hooking the fork,

I ticked five awful minutes by the hours,
Damned by the furious bubbles where they broke
Among my unwashed hands. And then I went
Up to the barn to find my mother cat.

We sat in a beam of sunlight on the floor
Petting and purring, while out of a knothole eye
Hung in the roof of God the motes of dust
Sang of our comforts and our curious loves.

Sacrifice of My Young Mare, Great with Colt

The blue guts of the evening
Spilled from the belly of God,
As I walked alone with my father
Across our grassy valley
And into the muddy bottoms.

Almost beyond believing,
A mudhole rimmed with rocks
Had swallowed our colt-great filly
Up to her bloated belly.
They swam together, rotting.

She was still alive, but heaving,
Choked in her muddy cud,
And I cried to my father, "Father,
What can we do?" "No telling.
Now she's going. We've lost one."

No rope or machine extending,
No stay of her heart or blood,
No hand outreached with power
Could help, or could even rally
The blasted day we were caught in.

I stood on that edge, deceiving
Myself that the swollen pod
Could spill itself in the quick-mud
And walk from our grassy valley
To the upland hills and the barn.

But her muddy death, upcreeping,
Swallowed the blood of her womb;
It crept on her foam-wet withers,
The bursting head overwhelming.
Then the last white eye, exploding,

Slipped under, beyond all seeing.
Caught there, in the belly of God
As I stood alone with my father,
I saw the blood of the mother
Bubble the pots of death.

They broke in dark circles, pleading
Completion in me. Unhoused,
The dark gods stood in the thickets.
My father said nothing. Aching,
I climbed the old slope toward home.

Sacrifice of the Old Gentleman

When our two great herd sires fought in the bur oak grove
Their bellows disturbed my sleep. I rolled in a heat
Of black hooves stomping the bottomlands, woke in a sweat,

Crying, "Mother, what is it?" Father and brothers were gone.
"I'm afraid," she said, "that our sires have broken out long
Ago in the night. Oh, I hope that nothing is wrong."

Our great Hereford bulls! Their fierce heads were as strong
As the iron bars of their gates, their bodies as thickly
Bound as the earth they stormed. I ran off quickly.

My father with bullwhip and gun, my brothers in boughs,
And I on a limb above them, all up in the oak,
Stared a short ways off. Their deep growls broke

And sank in a tunnel of throat. The foam-bloodied nose
Of one bull hung from his curls on a forehead of hot
Dust. And his loud dull eyes, bleared cannon shot,

Fell on the other's entrails, trampled in leaves.
There the Old Gentleman, Prince Bill, Second, The Great,
Growled his proud way toward death, his enormous weight

Plunged to the ground he had stalked and pawed and shook.
The horn wound in his side was the single eye
With which my brothers and I could watch him die.

It took both tractors and the neighbor's chains,
Ringing the country stones, to pull him down
Into that ditch where those awful weeds have grown.

His calves were gentle, and the cows he rode
Became more gentle. Still, his awesome head
Arose on the horns of war. Now he is dead.

He shook his anger and iron sex in a wreath
Of forehead curls. But when his deep-tongued breath
Exploded, he charged the trembling woods with death

And so located, stalking before his grave,
Dimensions of himself. Now, scrawny and weak,
Our crows and mourning doves and coyotes speak

Those tired themes which none of us escape.
Sighs, croaks, and howls beset our greatest voice
With common years of indiscriminate noise.

Sacrifice of the Old Sow

They said she was wild when the old sow ate the pigs
She farrowed into her straw in the stock-warm barn
Early in March. I caught her crunching the last
One in her jaws, then clung to the filthy patched
Gate and swallowed my breaking new-born tears.

My brother rushed at the sow, "You goddamn bitch,"
Jabbing his pitchfork in the bloodmother's flank;
"You devil, you goddamn devil," my brother screamed,
Trumpeting all the four ends of her pen
Wherever she crashed, "You bitch, you goddamn bitch."

I squeezed my eyes again at the rawest noise
Flung like manure on the squealing boards.
How could I know, my small hands to my heart,
That this huge barn-of-a-world was also stuffed
By Darwin and Marx and Freud at the feeding troughs?

And so, at last, there were only a hundred and twelve
Pigs to be raised. And since the old sow had fed
On the offspring she conceived, we strung her up
And slit her throat and stripped her down and ate
That succulent rib with which we kept alive.

Sacrifice of Eric

Missing our neighbor, we searched the empty sheds.
We called his name along the iced creek-beds.
Eric, we sang upon the rocky draws,
Eric, and then we faced the silent pause
With one ear cocked to the world.
                    Somehow, we knew,
But we kept pretense alive a day or two,
Following any tracks laid out in snow
Until we trailed ourselves in the moonglow.
And all that time, in woods by the gravel beds,
He stood in his swollen postures over our heads,
Hanging, frozen, and swinging free in air.
We stopped, a few feet off, too baffled there
To talk or move. Someone took off his hat.

Well, he was found. At least, we had done that.

Who got my neighbor there upon that limb?
      All those dark faces murmuring at his back?
Who slipped the latest noose that carried him?
      Did he? We looked; there was no other track.
Who quickened the thicket clutching at our clothes?
      Did he? The woodlands quaked upon our cries.
And who could read the winter's tale he knows?
      We saw that pale abyss, the unlidded eyes.
Who swung him out and downward from that bough?
      Did he? For fear our hanging hearts would break
We cut him down. Who bears his burden now?
      Who swings us all? Forbear, for Jesus' sake.

Toward those intolerable silences we came,
And action saved us when the mind was lame.
We tried some magic for an old complaint
And bowed.
            I thought some medieval saint
Stepped gently from the wounded wood which bore
Old Eric like a gargoyle evermore
And gave him, with eroded hands, a crown.

But seeing it wasn't so, we let him down
And carried him out across our bottomlands,
The deadweight of his world upon our hands,
And heard, and hear, in sudden solitudes,
An old wind walking in our lower woods.

I call him my own neighbor, when I dare,
But that's not easy, having come from there.

Sacrifice of Aunt Marie

My anemic aunt was alone in her flower garden
(Roses, petunias, wealthies, foxcomb and phlox)
On a Fourth of July that always seems fragrant with bloom,
When all of her nephews crept from the north of her house
(Cherries and winesaps, spearmint and red four-o'clocks)
And threw their firearms round in a crackerjack boom.

None of us looked, but Oh with what brilliance we ran
(Jellies and jonathans, peppermint, lilacs and mums)
And perched on our naughtiest wits by the Bear Creek rocks
And laughed till the sun set. Then we went back to look
(Thornwood, bleeding hearts, bittersweet, currants and plums),
And three days later we lowered her down in a box.

The old ladies patted us gently upon our heads
(Laces and liniment, cosmos and hoarhounds and thyme)
Where we sat alone in the shade of her northernmost doors.
The old men nodded and slyly glanced at their clocks
(Oh, gardens of heartsease, rainbowing honey of time),
And when we grew up we all went off to the wars.

V

The dark tides of the world
tell, with a bell of tongues,
    the inland sea.

The Amalfi Grotto

Water is light. It blooms from dipping oars
    In huge lilies with golden tongues
        Echoing in green caves,
            A lost home.
Even stalactites sing of sudden jewels
    Dropping from bright eyes.

Just for a moment, let us dispel this charm.
The sun plunged down far undersea
Enters this cave, reflects,
Surprising us
Upon these emerald waters. Filtered light
Illuminates this world.

We cup our hands among the waves of light.
    We drip a quick florescence from
        Our watery fingers. Bells
            Ring from our arms.
The fleeting ghost of daylight everywhere
    Taps on the bone of night.

I walked on water in a field of light
    And heard the dark tides of the world
        Tell, with a bell of tongues,
            The inland sea.
I do not tell you all. But who can be
    Complete with miracles?

In 1912, My Father Buys the Victor Record of "Sextet from Lucia" from Hoegh's Jewelry Store in a Small Town in Minnesota

Charley is entering the record and jewelry store now, a dapper forty-one, just married to his elegant Clara, with nine children still to be conceived and carried and born and raised clear into the Depression. He has just come from the bank, smartly dressed in his tight waistcoat and dark striped trousers. As he enters the door, Ove Hoegh glances up with appreciation: a favorite, a good customer, a friend.

Yes, indeed, he has some new records from the operas: Alma Gluck, some more Caruso, Louise Homer, Journet, Amati, even Melba, and a new quartet from *Rigoletto*. But Charley, I want you to hear this! Ove winds the Victrola, shining in polished oak. My father leans lightly against the jeweled counter and stands on his left foot, with his right balanced across it on the tip of its toe; his right elbow is on the counter, his left hand in his pocket. His head turns slightly outward into the room; he tips it ever so slightly down for listening.

Then the seven-dollar twelve-inch seventy-eight with its red-and-gold heart begins to turn. The shining steel needle, with a soft swish, slowly negotiates the black edge into the deep grooves, and the arpeggio chordal plucking in the strings begins. And then the huge horn hidden in the box behind its fine brocade begins softly singing: sol sol SOL, do MI re DO SOL in its vibrant Italian vowels. The little gallery is transfixed. Waves of harmonic melodies float up and over, interweave, making their exits and entering again with violins and rapiers and satin gowns. All their songs gesture in embroidered pantaloons and waxed moustaches; pale hands sweep over their troubled foreheads; they implore the air; they brace themselves on their hips, indignant, wan, robust, judicious, serene, over the carved table and the velvet and leather chairs.

Oh, my father is a fine man now, there in that royal box
with all that splendid company! His skull is the
philharmonic of them all, jeweled with sound.

And when intermission comes, he will step out on Main
Street and all along down Division, to greet his Clara
Elizabeth with an amulet under his arms to tell her, like a
messenger from on high, that La Scala has finally come—
Sembrich, Caruso, Scotti, Journet, Severina and Daddi—all
the way from Milano to Spring Grove, Minnesota, and he is
bringing them home.

Ballad in a Summer Season

Over the valley hills
of Iowa
slowly the darkness fills
all of the draws.

Down from the hanging sky
one star or two
falls from the jeweled night
like morning dew.

Summer is gentle now,
daylight a dream;
grass is a kingdom here,
hope is a queen.

Sheep in the bottomland,
cows by the barn,
all of my windows are
open at noon.

If you still love me now,
shed, house and barn,
I am still bold enough
to keep you warm.

Knock at my ready breast,
toll my heart-bell;
all of my valley sleeps
under this hill.

Fall of Icarus: Brueghel

Flashing through falling sunlight
A frantic leg late plunging from its strange
Communicating moment
Flutters in shadowy waves.

Close by those shattered waters—
The spray, no doubt, struck shore—
One dreamless shepherd and his old sheep dog
Define outrageous patience
Propped on staff and haunches,
Intent on nothing, backs bowed against the sea,
While the slow flocks of sheep gnaw on the grass-thin coast.
Crouched in crimson homespun an indifferent peasant
Guides his blunt plow through gravelled ground,
Cutting flat furrows hugging this hump of land.
One partridge sits immobile on its bough
Watching a Flemish fisherman pursue
Fish in the darkening bay;
Their stillness mocks rude ripples rising and circling in.

Yet that was a stunning greeting
For any old angler, peasant, or the grand ship's captain,
Though sent by a mere boy
Bewildered in the gravitational air,
Flashing his wild white arms at the impassive sea-drowned sun.

Now only coastal winds
Ruffle the partridge feathers,
Muting the soft ripping of sheep cropping,
The heavy whisper
Of furrows falling, ship cleaving,
Water lapping.

Lulled in the loose furl and hum of infamous folly,
Darkly, how silently, the cold sea suckles him.

Hunters in the Snow: Brueghel

Quail and rabbit hunters with tawny hounds,
Shadowless, out of late afternoon
Trudge toward the neutral evening of indeterminate form.
Done with their blood-annunciated day
Public dogs and all the passionless mongrels
Through deep snow
Trail their deliberate masters
Descending from the upper village home in hovering light.
Sooty lamps
Glow in the stone-carved kitchens.

This is the fabulous hour of shape and form
When Flemish children are gray-black-olive
And green-dark-brown
Scattered and skating informal figures
On the mill ice pond.
Moving in stillness
A hunched dame struggles with her bundled sticks,
Letting her evening's comfort cudgel her
While she, like jug or wheel, like a wagon cart
Walked by lazy oxen along the old snowlanes,
Creeps and crunches down the dusky street.
High in the fire-red dooryard
Half unhitched the sign of the Inn
Hangs in wind
Tipped to the pitch of the roof.
Near it anonymous parents and peasant girl,
Living like proverbs carved in the alehouse walls,
Gather the country evening into their arms
And lean to the glowing flames.

Now in the dimming distance fades
The other village; across the valley
Imperturbable Flemish cliffs and crags
Vaguely advance, close in, loom
Lost in nearness. Now
The night-black raven perched in branching boughs
Opens its early wing and slipping out

Above the gray-green valley
Weaves a net of slumber over the snow-capped homes.
And now the church, and then the walls and roofs
Of all the little houses are become
Close kin to shadow with small lantern eyes.
And now the bird of evening
With shadows streaming down from its gliding wings
Circles the neighboring hills
Of Hertogenbosch, Brabant.

Darkness stalks the hunters,
Slowly sliding down,
Falling in beating rings and soft diagonals.
Lodged in the vague vast valley the village sleeps.

Henri Matisse

Discrimination through pure color
Is one sure way to shock
New admirations from the universal heart.

Anaphoras of sound, another.
And proud angular lines
Circling upon the dancing of their own rhythms.

If blue ladies sleep on a green couch
In a green room, dreaming
Beyond yellow roses and pink blinds to the clear

Blue Mediterranean, dreaming
As far as eyes can dream
Beyond those bedroom windows, then one red petal

Reflects on the mirrors of the sea,
A floating miracle
Flaming upon that subtle and watery world

And all clear. We were, you know, in dreams:
Blue ladies somnolent,
Yellow roses in vases silent as roses—

And then, psst, Monsieur Henri Matisse
Looked at his world and said,
I'm lonely, and in his own image created

The green ennui of Eden, mild blue
Skies, and sleeping ladies
Arousing their blue heads under his apple boughs.

Sibelius

It is nine-thirty in the morning. On the phonograph Colin Davis is leading the Boston Symphony in the Fifth Symphony of Sibelius when I particularly notice a single chord. It is one of the many moments in that great Finn when, after some fairly vigorous explorations in the brass and woodwind sections, filled in with heavy drumming, it seems that they are all seeking some harmonious home. Then something momentarily resolves, and there, yah! the chord is. Yah! Large, rich, fulfilled, and then held.

The strings shimmer around it; the timpani keep up, pianissimo, their almost imperceptible vibrato. The sun floods in the windows. Everyone in the house stops talking. One can even hear the teakettle humming in the kitchen. Outside, the snow lies under the winter birches, radiant and white, and on the porch railing one small icicle gives off, if you see it just right, a fleeting spectrum of the rainbow. For maybe all of ten or twenty seconds you simply stand there in the house, your mouth slightly open, your eyes looking nowhere, and just do not breathe.

Then Jan, the old Finn, lets out a blast on the trombone; the horns shout wildly; the woodwinds pick up the echoes and swirl in high excitement, and the violins in chorus follow in full pursuit over the next hill. Everybody in the house starts talking again, all at once.

Yah! Spring is coming!

Upon Hearing Three Hundred Children Singing

in Jonathan Edwards's Church,
Northampton, 5 March 1961

I heard three hundred children singing sweetly together,
Cleanly in robes, their bright eyes looking at heaven,
And their voices floating out of their innocent faces
Under the nave. High under the chancel windows
They met the rainbowing sun, and they sang together.

I heard three hundred children marching along together
With hearts all gay and their shapely mouths all smiling,
And over and under and through them the great bass organ
Ground out processional laws in the modes of their sermons,
Delivered in chorus before all their mothers and fathers.

Three hundred children, all singing under those shadows,
Admonished the devil, and all in the clearest soprano
Roaming the vales of our tears with a jubilant leisure
Under the stern director. But under the shadows
The pipes blew faintly in forests beyond their meadows.

Hearing three hundred children singing so sweetly together
I remembered that once I was singing, so many together,
And the sanctifications were lost in a fable of Sundays
And fabulous Mondays; and yet I was glad to be chanting
In such casual guises as now I am nevermore singing.

I heard three hundred children ascending the hymns and
                    carols
While fathers and mothers sat in their dark rows, smiling,
And thought: how delightful, innocent, charming and
                    proper
It is for our children to sing, who must walk through
                    shadows
And the long long valleys upward to mothers and fathers.

I heard three hundred children communing at decorous
             altars.
I forget what they sang (maybe something as glossy as
             morals)
But their faces shone in their songs, and I dreamt that evils
Foregathered among them and stalked around in their
             singing,
But still they sang on to sons and their sons' generations.

I heard three hundred children wound in the wisdom of ages
And all of them cheery about the dark words they were
             chanting,
Yet clever enough for their words. Oh, their minds so clearly
Moved with the music and sun I forgot they were singing,
Being father and son and grandson and greatgrandfather

Hearing three hundred children at play in the heavenly
             chancels
And three hundred children at song in the blossoming
             meadows
And Adam at morning out walking with Eve by the apples.

A Madrigal: For Judith

Smooth patios in shadow call us out
    Further into the sun
      Until our homes
Flower beyond our present laugh and shout
    Into the southern woodlands;

As evening waits upon the sunlight there,
    Dusk edges up the trunks
      Of trees and moves
Across all hollows, draws, invading where
    Frail copper bells of leaves

Dangle in pale designs. Skirting the long
    Meadows open to sun,
      One golden plunge
Over the precipice concludes this song
    And all its shadowy loves.

Among Olive Groves: Montepertuso

This moment keeps its marble distances,
But in those distances the olive trees
Vaguely diffuse in parables of green;
They root our silences, defend the slopes,
And back the mountain with a silver sleep.

Sunk in our teeth the olive's bitterness,
Tangy and raw, untutored in its boughs,
Puckers the sucking lips, curdles our speech
And drives such parables against the brain
As will defile it. Save that memory.

Hauled on the hearth the knotted yellow wood
Quickens a golden tongue. Under a plane
Baroquely serpentining grains emerge,
A torture of design, while on our back
Hangs excommunication like a whip

Of thorn and spear-heart leaf at one remove,
One doveflight from the world. Small distances
Transport the olive into gracefulness
Where Jesus in our gold beatitudes
Dispensed his talents with analogies.

Those leaves were green, subtle and dull and green;
They spoke of gracile otherwheres to all
Who mused among their angularities.
If chaos brought the olive to that light,
Will broken honor raise the soul at last

And court it from this pale solicitude?
I look for signs among the olive trees.
A greeny leaf is there, a bitter fruit,
Gray twisted limbs, strange airy attitudes,
And prophets dreaming in the ancient groves.

Rocky Mountain Snowstorm

Loined in lean wind
The white panther
Coils and roars
At the human strangers.

Dry chill whips
This world's good-morrow.
Love is a raging cat
At natural zero.

Stalking our wild land
Mad winter stiffens
Herd and man
With definition;

While from our tiny windows
And civil plans
We watch the snow-white panther
Ravish dead land.

Housed from desperate passion,
Half warmed, we sit
Shivering, complaining,
Bogged in wit,

Scarcely aware, beholding
This wild unrest,
Of the lean destroyer thawing
The stony breast.

Walden

When I first went to Walden Pond
alone in the afternoon of the last day of summer
in the centennial of his death
the woods rang with sparrows, squirrels and crows.
Turning around the rockpile of Thoreau's hut
I discovered, also, that I had been born
in the centennial of his birth.
There in the lifted day, Icarian bird,
I circled the dark edge of an ancient dream
and started down to the water.

And the very first person I met upon my path
was a tall young Negro.
He stood easily by the woodsy pond
with his white girl friend,
casually linking their hands by a leaning birch.
Its leaves quivered in a light breeze
wakening over the dark waters,
and under the random clouds in that deep sky
we smiled, and I went on.

And the very next person I met upon that path
was a brown man from India
lounging in mottled pebbles and blond sand
with a college sweatshirt hung on his shoulders.
Into that lake he dipped his golden hands;
he turned his palms in the common water
and lifted them, all spangled,
in the mystical geometry of light.
Drops fell in a chain
and linked their circular furrows on the pond.
A frog plunked from the bank;
an autumn leaf swung down.
A blue jay screamed;
we smiled, and I went on.

And further along the brightly shadowed woods
the very next person I met upon that path
was a wild white man
running and leaping through the brush,
mumbling some half-hummed song as he ran.
His jacket was flung open;
his face shone with light;
and a rumpled paisley muffler of rainbowing colors
trailed from his torn pocket
and waved
in floating arcs among the aisles of trees,
frightening the song sparrows into sudden answers
as he fled on.

And then, at a further turn, I met myself.
I smiled and stepped to the tall and weedy shades
at the small bay on the western edge,
stripped to my native self
on brackish ground and shining sand
and, walking into the sun from tufted sedge
past polliwogs, mud flats and water spiders,
I strode those slippery shoals to the clear blue
and dove in calm delight
to thrash my limbs and throw my pale white arms
around those springing waters.

Seeing the afternoon break from the woods
I heard the long dark tale of history flashing down
and rose in a clear dream.
Simply jeweled with all that pond
I put my homely raiment on
and rode the luminous hum of the blue-gray twilight
through Concord, all the way back
to my Amherst American home.

Libertyville

for Adlai

The state tree, bird and flower of Illinois
are the oak, cardinal and violet

There is a fountain in a wood
and by the fountain a green oak,
and in the oak a cardinal,
and near the oak's abiding root
a leaf and flower of violet.
And if the elder oak be green,
the redbird's whistle clear in tone
and the low violet sweet in bloom,
that's half a rainbow, but the rest
      depends on us.

There is a river in that wood
of sky-blue water, and a disk
of midnight sun and midday moon;
if any traveler, looking out
from the deep shadow of his mind,
can tell what banks to lie upon
and drink beyond confusion,
      that's half a rainbow.

There is a flower at the edge
of the blue water. In the oak
the sun and moon have built a nest;
and in that nest, you may have heard,
there is a bird, there is a bird.
And in his beak there is a leaf.
Now in the morning of a death
I dream of Noah, riding high
upon some possibility
toward Africa and Everest.
But that's a rainbow. And the tale
is fragmentary. Still, the rest
      depends . . .

VI

scarcely hearing the apocalypse
galloping away in the shadows.

A Dream of Love

Once upon a time
three brothers kept three horses
in a farmyard near a forest not far from a magnificent castle.
According to the old story,
one was black, one brown, and one white.
Each night one of the brothers caught his own horse in the
                early evening,
and in the glimmering darkness
he tried to ride it up a great glass hill
into that fairy kingdom.

And somewhere three beautiful horses,
with stars just under their forelocks
and hooves aglow in the moonlight,
nicker out of my childhood
and neigh in the distant meadows.
They stand at night in the pastures
with Bell and King and Beauty,
with Czar and Kate by the river
munching the grass by the timber
in the hills of northeastern Iowa,
with Blossom and Queen and Noble
wild in the harness of springtime,
tame in the woodland of summer;
with May and June, gray-dappled,
mild in their stalls in the winter,
trotting with sleighs and wagons,
straining at tugs in the snowdrifts,
farting out loud in the village,
working and sweating and sleeping;
with Roxy and Trixy and Mabel,
biting and pawing and snorting
when led to the western stallion,
ears flat on their foreheads, breeding,
their nostrils flaring, kicking,
till their hind legs set like pillars;
with Daisy and Bill and Lady
chucking for oats in the morning,

chortling for hay in the evening,
and at county fairs with sulkies
racing with silver jockeys
and galloping over the hillsides.

My hands still fiddle with those bridles still,
the steel bits sliding over the white shining teeth,
past the dark elastic lips and pink tongues
swallowing into their soft throats.
I pull the reins taut; my arms tighten on their sleek muscles,
and again the polished hooves go clattering
out of the moonlit barnyard and on to the glass hill
where the breathless lady waits with her gossamer gowns
            and pale lips, chill as the night,
for the breath of her one true lover.

Daisy and Lady and Beauty,
we curry your hair in the morning,
your manes in the morning combing,
braiding your tails in the morning,
your velvet nostrils rubbing,
your rumps all silken, slapping;
on your barrel backs still climbing
I bury my face in your manes.
I snuggle my crotch on your withers,
my legs on your rib-flanks wrapping
to touch my feet to your belly.
And we walk and trot and gallop
out of the barns to the roadway
and up the road to the mailbox
and over the hills to the neighbors,
then back again to the barnyard
where I clean your stalls of manure
and bed you down for the evening
in bundles of golden straw.

Black Beauty, I think, is still whinnying in the orchards and
            weeping by waterfalls.
Postilions, coaches and schooners are running wild in their
            old tracks.

Flicka has tossed her tail up again west of Cheyenne and is
    headed into the mountains.
Smoky the Cowhorse is languishing in his harness,
trying to make that shriveled heart grow back again to full
    size.
The Red Pony and spotted horses are asleep in the
    bookshelves,
and Rosa Bonheur has scribbled magnificent horses all over
    the one-room schoolhouse wall.

Horses are standing by roadways,
charging over the sagebrush
in their oiled and studded saddles;
they are swimming the swollen rivers
through Wyoming, leaping and bucking
and plunging in dust storms of cattle;
Old Paint is off to Montana,
walking the tourists in mountains
and standing by livery stables
and threshing grain on the prairies.

And somewhere in the local theaters of Spring Grove,
    Minnesota, and Decorah, Iowa,
legions of horses are rising and leaping out of the wild
    Atlantic
onto the Brittany beaches.
Their seaweed manes are rising and falling, their hooves
rising and falling, the wind-driven grass rising
and falling over the dunes,
and the dark French rustlers with their stiff black hats
are throwing silver lariats everywhere out of the hills.

And the Good Men are riding their horses,
and the Bad Men riding their horses,
the stagecoach is whipping its horses,
and the Indians are riding their horses,
and the Tartars are riding their horses,
and Genghis Khan and the Chinese
emperors riding their horses.

And horses are guarding the palace,
and Lawrence is riding his horses
with all his Arabians running
to the muffled drums of the sand.

And the great blue horses of Franz Marc
stand in Bavaria near Benedicktbüren with their strict
                        geometric rumps,
and Dutch horses wait near courtyards fat as burghers.
By the hay wains set by streams, horses are no more than a
                        mound or a lamp post.
And where is that young blue Spanish boy with his elegant
                        mare?
Are they dreaming of blankets of flowers
falling over the pastel horses charging through steeplechases
                        out of the suburbs of Paris?
Or the cavalry milling by Moscow, the horses like dreary
                        plains?
Or horses like trumpets and bugles falling, bloodstained, out
                        of the sky?

There are princes arriving on chargers
and departing, forever and ever,
where the farm boys sleep with their horses,
and horses hidden in thickets
while the cavalry passes on horses,
and horses pressed against boulders
while the posse passes on horses,
and horses stilled in the hemlocks
while the murderers spur at their horses,
and the hunters go by on their horses
past rivers and castles and mountains.

And still the corporal is rearing upon his stallion in the
                        Louvre,
and the generals sit stiffly astride their bronze studs
in all the public squares of Europe,
and Xanthus sulks with Achilles,
and Pegasus rides from the sea foam,

Al Borak carries Mohammed,
Bucephalus, Alexander,
and Sleipnir trots with Odin
out of the fjords to the ocean;
then out of the long processional friezes
where the marble horses twist and prance for the proud
               cities
Apollo rides straight up like thunder into the skies.

And the horses are fled in the passes
with the horn of Roland winding
and Charlemagne riding his horses
and Joan of Arc at the crossroads
and the highwaymen riding their horses.
Brazilian horses are running,
and the listener sits in the moonlight,
alone on his horse in the moonlight,
with his horse in a dream forever.
Eohippus sleeps in the lavas;
and the Hittites' horses are running;
Mesohippus sleeps in the lavas;
the Persian horses are running.
In the steppes the horses are plunging
with stars just under their forelocks;
they are galloping over the tundra;
they are leaping from mountain to mountain
with hooves aglow in the moonlight.
They have harnessed the waves of the ocean.
They are riding up over our beaches.
They are running wild in our cities.
I love you! I love you!

And then the brown horse and the black horse and the white
               horse
leaped so high in the moonlight that when they came back
               down
there was only a dappled one,
and he floated up out of the back pastures over the hills of
               northeastern Iowa.

And when he came to your garden
where you sat in a blue dress on a pallet on the lawn
his hooves rang like polished bells,
and he knelt on his silken hocks and knees by your side,
laid his slender head gently upon your lap,
looked up at your face with his marble eye,
then folded the silver membrane of his eyelid down,
and slept,
scarcely hearing the apocalypse
galloping away in the shadows.